Growing Together in Faith

A Year of Prayer for Christian Couples

Faye & Henry Smith

Little AP Publishing

Contents

Introduction

Welcome to *Growing Together in Faith: A Year of Prayer for Christian Couples*. We are delighted to embark on this transformative journey with you as we explore the profound power of prayer within the context of marriage. This book is designed to be your companion on a year-long adventure, a voyage that will strengthen the bond between you and your spouse, deepen your connection to God, and fortify the foundation of your Christian marriage.

The institution of marriage is a sacred covenant, a divine union established by God Himself. It is a lifelong commitment that invites us to love, cherish, and support one another through all of life's joys and challenges. As Christian couples, we are called to live out our marriage vows with unwavering faith, guided by the teachings of Jesus Christ and sustained by prayer.

Prayer is a cornerstone of the Christian faith, a direct line of communication with our Heavenly Father. It is through prayer that we seek God's guidance, find strength in times of weakness, and experience the transformative power of His love. When a husband and wife come together in prayer, they invite the presence of God into their relationship, allowing Him to be the anchor that holds them steady through the storms of life.

Throughout the next 52 weeks, you and your spouse will embark on a remarkable journey of spiritual growth, personal reflection, and shared devotion. Each week, we will explore a different aspect of married life, from communication and trust to intimacy and financial stewardship. Together, we will delve into the wisdom of Scripture, engage in meaningful conversations, and participate in practical exercises that will draw you closer to each other and God.

We hope that *Growing Together in Faith* will not only serve as a guide but also as a source of inspiration and renewal for your marriage. As you commit to praying together, you will discover the profound impact it can have on your relationship. You will learn to navigate the challenges of life as a united front, and you will celebrate the blessings and joys that come with a shared faith.

Throughout this journey, remember that God is with you every step of the way. He rejoices in your commitment to each other and your desire to seek His presence together. Your marriage is a unique and beautiful expression of His love, and through prayer, you will find strength, wisdom, and grace to nurture it.

So, let us begin this year of prayer with open hearts, eager minds, and a deep sense of gratitude for the gift of marriage. May God's presence be felt in every moment, and may your love for one another grow stronger with each passing day. Together, let us embark on this sacred journey of *Growing Together in Faith*, knowing that with God at the center, our marriages can flourish and thrive beyond our wildest dreams.

Week 1: Building The Foundation

In the first week of our journey, we focus on laying a solid foundation for your marriage through prayer. Just as a building needs a strong and stable foundation to withstand the test of time, so does a marriage. We invite you and your spouse to come together in prayer to seek God's guidance and blessings for your life together.

Prayer Prompt:

Dear Heavenly Father,

We come before you as a married couple, acknowledging your role as the cornerstone of our relationship. Just as you are the foundation of our faith, we ask that you be the foundation of our marriage. Strengthen the bonds of love and commitment between us. Grant us the wisdom to build our lives on the solid rock of your teachings, and may our union be a testimony of your grace and love to the world. In Jesus' name, we pray. Amen.

Scripture Reflection:

- Matthew 7:24-25 (NIV)
  "Therefore everyone who hears these words of mine and puts them into practice is like a wise man who built his house on the rock. The rain came down, the streams rose, and the winds blew and beat against that house; yet it did not fall because it had its foundation on the rock."

Discussion Questions:

1. How do you envision your marriage as a strong and stable "house" built on a solid foundation?

2. What are some key principles from the Bible that you believe should form the foundation of your marriage?

3. How can you both actively apply these principles in your daily lives?

Activities:

1. Create a "Marriage Vision Statement" together, outlining your shared goals, values, and aspirations for your marriage.

2. Discuss and write down your individual strengths and areas where you can support each other in building a stronger foundation.

3. Start a journal where you both can record your thoughts, prayers, and reflections throughout this year-long journey.

Week 2: Communicating and Understanding

E ffective communication is essential for any successful marriage. It's through open and honest conversations that couples connect, resolve conflicts, and grow together. In Week 2, we will focus on praying for improved communication and understanding between you and your spouse.

Prayer Prompt:

Dear Lord,

We come before you with gratitude for the gift of communication. Help us to use our words to build each other up, to listen with patience and empathy, and to speak with love and kindness. May our communication be a reflection of your grace and understanding. In Jesus' name, we pray. Amen.

Scripture Reflection:

- Ephesians 4:29 (NIV)
  "Do not let any unwholesome talk come out of your mouths, but only what is helpful for building others up according to their needs, that it may benefit those who listen."

Discussion Questions:

1. What are some communication challenges you've faced in your marriage, and how have they affected your relationship?

2. How can you apply the principles of Ephesians 4:29 to your communication with each other?

3. What steps can you take to actively improve your communication and understanding?

Activities:

1. Set aside dedicated time each day to have a meaningful conversation with your spouse, focusing on open and honest communication.

2. Practice active listening by summarizing and validating each other's feelings during conversations.

3. Read a book or article together to enhance your communication skills.

Suggested   article:
https://tacomachristiancounseling.com/articles/how-to-communicate-b
etter-gods-way#:~:text=everyone%20should%20be%20quick%20to,not%
20ended%20by%20multiplying%20words%2C

Week 3: Deepening Your Connection through Communication

Week 3 delves even deeper into the essential aspect of communication within your marriage, with a focus on deepening your connection through effective and empathetic communication. Communication is the cornerstone of a healthy and thriving relationship, and this week, you will explore ways to enhance your connection through meaningful conversations.

Prayer Prompt:

Heavenly Father,

As we embrace the importance of communication, we seek your wisdom and guidance. Help us to communicate with love and understanding, deepening our connection as a couple. May our words and actions reflect your love and grace. In Jesus' name, we pray. Amen.

Scripture Reflection:

- Proverbs 16:24 (NIV)
  "Gracious words are a honeycomb, sweet to the soul and healing to the bones."

Discussion Questions:

1. Reflect on your current communication patterns as a couple. What are some strengths and areas for growth?

2. Share examples of moments when effective communication deepened your connection. What contributed to those positive experiences?

3. How can you apply the message of Proverbs 16:24, emphasizing the sweetness and healing power of gracious words, to your commitment to enhancing your connection through communication?

Activities:

1. Work together to identify what makes each other feel comfortable to be open for deeper communication.

2. Set aside designated times for open and honest communication, where you discuss your joys, concerns, and aspirations.

3. Create a list of discussion topics or questions that promote meaningful conversations, and take turns exploring them together.

Week 4: Trust and Forgiveness

T rust and forgiveness are vital components of a healthy and thriving marriage. This week, we will pray for the cultivation of trust in your relationship and the strength to offer and receive forgiveness when needed.

Prayer Prompt:

Gracious Father,

We acknowledge that trust and forgiveness are essential elements of a strong marriage. Help us to trust each other wholeheartedly and to forgive as you have forgiven us. May our marriage be a haven where trust is unwavering, and forgiveness flows freely. In Jesus' name, we pray. Amen.

Scripture Reflection:

- Colossians 3:13 (NIV)
  "Bear with each other and forgive one another if any of you has a grievance against someone. Forgive as the Lord forgave you."

Discussion Questions:

1. What does trust mean to you in the context of your marriage, and how can it be strengthened?

2. Share a personal experience of forgiveness, either given or received and its impact on your relationship.

3. How can you apply the teachings of Colossians 3:13 to your marriage when facing conflicts or hurtful situations?

Activities:

1. Write down any past grievances or misunderstandings, and then discuss and forgive each other for these issues.

2. Set boundaries and expectations together to build and maintain trust in your marriage.

3. Set aside time for eye gazing sessions: Sit facing each other, preferably with your knees touching. Close your eyes and take a deep breath; when you are ready open your eyes. Look into each other's eyes without breaking eye contact for a pre-determined amount of time (5 minutes is a good time to begin with, you can use a

timer). After a minute or so has passed, softly compliment each other while maintaining eye contact. Allow the conversation to continue where it does while maintaining eye contact until the time has passed.

Week 5: Forgiveness

In Week 5, we explore the essential topics of forgiveness in marriage. Conflicts are a natural part of any relationship, and learning how to resolve them healthily is key to maintaining a strong and loving marriage.

Prayer Prompt:

Dear Lord,

As we delve into learning forgiveness, we seek your wisdom and guidance. Grant us the strength to resolve conflicts with love and grace, and the capacity to forgive as you have forgiven us. May our marriage be a testament to your reconciling love. In Jesus' name, we pray. Amen.

Scripture Reflection:

- Colossians 3:13 (NIV)
  "Bear with each other and forgive one another if any of you has a grievance against someone. Forgive as the Lord forgave you."

Discussion Questions:

1. Reflect on your approach to conflict resolution in your marriage. What strategies have worked well, and where can you improve?

2. Share experiences of forgiveness within your relationship. How has forgiveness strengthened your marriage?

3. How can you apply the message of Colossians 3:13, emphasizing forgiveness as the Lord forgave, to your commitment to resolving conflicts and extending forgiveness to each other?

Activities:

1. Practice conflict resolution techniques such as active listening, compromise, and seeking common ground during a role-playing exercise.

2. Dedicate a specific time to discuss past conflicts that have been resolved successfully, and analyze what contributed to their resolution.

3. Exchange written apologies or letters of forgiveness to express your love and commitment to reconciling after disagreements.

Week 6: Trust and Transparency

Week 6 focuses on the foundational principles of trust and transparency in a Christian marriage. Trust is a cornerstone of a healthy relationship, and being transparent with one another fosters openness and vulnerability.

Prayer Prompt:

Gracious Father,

As we explore the importance of trust and transparency, we seek your guidance. Help us to build and maintain trust in our marriage, and grant us the courage to be transparent with one another. May our marriage be a reflection of your truth and love. In Jesus' name, we pray. Amen.

Scripture Reflection:

- Proverbs 3:5-6 (NIV)

  "Trust in the Lord with all your heart and lean not on your own understanding; in all your ways submit to him, and he will make your paths straight."

Discussion Questions:

1. Reflect on the level of trust and transparency in your marriage. What actions can you take to strengthen these foundations?

2. Share moments when the trust was tested and transparency was essential. How did you navigate those situations, and what did you learn?

3. How can you apply the message of Proverbs 3:5-6, emphasizing trust in the Lord, to your commitment to trust and transparency in your marriage?

Activities:

1. Engage in trust-building exercises or games that foster openness and vulnerability, such as sharing your dreams or fears.

2. Write down personal affirmations of trust and transparency that you can exchange and reflect upon during moments of doubt or challenge.

3. Dedicate a special time for an open and honest conversation,

where you both express your commitment to trust and transparency and discuss ways to strengthen these foundations.

Week 7: Gratitude and Appreciation

In Week 7, we explore the significance of gratitude and appreciation in your marriage. Expressing thankfulness for one another and acknowledging the blessings in your relationship can deepen your love and connection.

Prayer Prompt:

Dear Lord,

As we focus on gratitude and appreciation, we invite your presence into our hearts and marriage. Help us to cultivate a spirit of thankfulness and to express our love and appreciation for each other daily. May our marriage be filled with gratitude and love. In Jesus' name, we pray. Amen.

Scripture Reflection:

- 1 Thessalonians 5:18 (NIV)
  "Give thanks in all circumstances; for this is God's will for you in
  Christ Jesus."

Discussion Questions:

1. Reflect on your current practices of expressing gratitude and appreciation in your marriage. What are some ways you can enhance
   them?

2. Share moments when you felt deeply appreciated or grateful for
   your spouse. How did those moments strengthen your bond?

3. How can you apply the message of 1 Thessalonians 5:18, emphasizing giving thanks in all circumstances, to your commitment to
   cultivating gratitude and appreciation in your marriage?

Activities:

1. Begin a gratitude journal or notebook where you both write down
   things you appreciate about each other daily or weekly.

2. Set aside a dedicated time each day or week to express gratitude
   and appreciation verbally or through written notes.

3. Create a list of personalized "love language" actions or gestures
   that make each of you feel especially appreciated and loved, and
   commit to incorporating them into your daily lives.

Week 8: Growing Together in Faith

Introduction:

In Week 8, we will delve deeper into the importance of growing together in faith as a couple. Your spiritual journey is a vital aspect of your marriage, and nurturing it can lead to a deeper connection with each other and with God.

Prayer Prompt:

Gracious Father,

As we explore the significance of growing together in faith, we ask for your guidance and blessings. Help us cultivate a shared spiritual journey that strengthens our love for you and each other. May our faith be the foundation of our marriage. In Jesus' name, we pray. Amen.

Scripture Reflection:

- Ecclesiastes 4:12 (NIV)
"Though one may be overpowered, two can defend themselves. A cord of three strands is not quickly broken."

Discussion Questions:

1. Reflect on your individual spiritual journeys and how they have influenced your marriage. How can you grow together in faith?

2. Share any specific spiritual practices or rituals you'd like to incorporate as a couple.

3. How can you apply the message of Ecclesiastes 4:12, emphasizing the strength of a threefold cord, to your commitment to growing together in faith?

Activities:

1. Attend a church service or spiritual event together, discussing your thoughts and insights afterward.

2. Set aside time for joint Bible study or devotional reading, selecting a passage or topic that resonates with both of you.

3. Write down your personal spiritual goals and aspirations, and discuss how you can support each other in achieving them.

Week 9: Nurturing Your Spiritual Connection

Week 9 is dedicated to nurturing your spiritual connection as a couple. Building a strong spiritual foundation can bring you closer to God and to each other, enhancing the depth of your marriage.

Prayer Prompt:

Dear Lord,

As we focus on nurturing our spiritual connection, we invite your presence into our hearts and marriage. Bless our efforts to grow closer to you and to strengthen our bond as a couple. May our love and faith continue to flourish. In Jesus' name, we pray. Amen.

Scripture Reflection:

- Colossians 3:17 (NIV)
  "And whatever you do, whether in word or deed, do it all in the name of the Lord Jesus, giving thanks to God the Father through him."

Discussion Questions:

1. Share your experiences of nurturing your spiritual connection thus far. What practices or moments have been particularly meaningful?

2. Discuss how you can incorporate prayer and scripture reading into your daily routines as a couple.

3. How can you apply the message of Colossians 3:17, emphasizing doing all things in the name of the Lord, to your commitment to nurturing your spiritual connection?

Activities:

1. Plan a special prayer night together, where you pray for each other's spiritual growth and any challenges you may be facing.

2. Create a list of scriptures or verses that hold personal significance for both of you, and reflect on them together.

3. Commit to a specific spiritual discipline or practice, such as fasting, meditation, or acts of service, and share your experiences and

insights as you implement it.

Week 10: A Prayer for Intimacy and Romance

Intimacy and romance are essential elements that keep the flame of love burning brightly in a marriage. In Week 10, we will focus on praying for the deepening of your emotional and physical connection as a couple.

Prayer Prompt:

Heavenly Father,

We thank you for the gift of intimacy and romance in our marriage. Help us to nurture the passion and affection between us. May our love continue to grow stronger, and may we find joy in the romantic moments we share. Bless our physical and emotional connection, and may it always be a reflection of your love for us. In Jesus' name, we pray. Amen.

Scripture Reflection:

- Song of Solomon 4:7 (NIV)
  "You are altogether beautiful, my darling; there is no flaw in you."

Discussion Questions:

1. How do you define intimacy in your marriage, and why is it important?

2. Share some of your favorite romantic moments or gestures within your relationship.

3. In what ways can you prioritize and enhance intimacy and romance in your daily lives?

Activities:

1. Plan a special date night together, complete with a romantic dinner, candlelight, and meaningful conversation.

2. Write love letters or notes to each other, expressing your feelings, desires, and appreciation.

3. Create a list of activities or hobbies you both enjoy and can do together to strengthen your emotional bond.

Week 11: Biblical Insights on Intimacy

God's Word provides profound insights into the sacredness of physical intimacy within marriage. In Week 11, we will delve into the Scriptures to gain a deeper understanding of God's design for intimacy and how it can strengthen your marital bond.

Prayer Prompt:

Dear Lord,

We seek your wisdom and guidance as we explore the biblical perspective on intimacy. Help us to honor your design for physical closeness within the boundaries of our marriage. May our intimacy be a source of unity, pleasure, and connection as we grow together in love. In Jesus' name, we pray. Amen.

Scripture Reflection:

- 1 Corinthians 7:3-5 (NIV)
  "The husband should fulfill his marital duty to his wife, and like-wise the wife to her husband. The wife does not have authority over her own body but yields it to her husband. In the same way, the husband does not have authority over his own body but yields it to his wife. Do not deprive each other except perhaps by mutual consent and for a time, so that you may devote yourselves to prayer. Then come together again so that Satan will not tempt you because of your lack of self-control."

Discussion Questions:

1. How does the Bible describe the role of physical intimacy within marriage?

2. What challenges, if any, have you faced in maintaining intimacy in your relationship, and how can you address them?

3. How can you apply the principles of 1 Corinthians 7:3-5 to your own marriage?

Activities:

1. Read and discuss passages from the Song of Solomon, exploring its poetic and symbolic descriptions of marital intimacy.

2. Share your personal views and desires regarding physical intimacy in your marriage, ensuring open and respectful communication.

3. Study books or resources that provide a biblical perspective on intimacy in marriage. (see Resources appendix for some suggestions)

Week 12: Nurturing Romance in Everyday Life

R omance is not confined to special occasions but can be woven into the fabric of everyday life. In Week 12, we will focus on practical ways to nurture romance and keep the spark alive in your marriage daily.

Prayer Prompt:

Heavenly Father,

We thank you for the gift of romance in our marriage. Help us to see the beauty in everyday moments and infuse our daily lives with love and affection. May we continually express our love for each other through small gestures and heartfelt words. In Jesus' name, we pray. Amen.

Scripture Reflection:

- Proverbs 5:18-19 (NIV)
  "May your fountain be blessed, and may you rejoice in the wife of your youth. A loving doe, a graceful deer—may her breasts satisfy you always, may you ever be intoxicated with her love."

Discussion Questions:

1. Share examples of everyday romantic gestures you have experienced or would like to incorporate into your marriage.

2. How can you maintain a sense of novelty and excitement in your relationship as time goes on?

3. What are some challenges that may hinder romance in your daily lives, and how can you overcome them?

Activities:

1. Create a list of everyday romantic gestures you can implement, such as leaving love notes, sharing compliments, or cooking a special meal together.

2. Surprise each other with unexpected acts of kindness and affection throughout the week.

3. Set aside dedicated time each day to connect emotionally, whether through conversation, a shared activity, or simply spending quality time together.

Week 13: Rekindling Passion in Marriage

Over time, the passion in marriage may ebb and flow, but it can always be rekindled with intention and effort. In Week 13, we will explore ways to reignite the flames of passion and keep the love alive in your relationship.

Prayer Prompt:

Loving Father,

We recognize that passion is a gift from you, and we seek your guidance in rekindling the fire of passion in our marriage. Help us to pursue each other with desire and cultivate a love that burns brightly through the years. May our physical and emotional connection continue to deepen and flourish. In Jesus' name, we pray. Amen.

Scripture Reflection:

- Song of Solomon 7:10 (NIV):

"I belong to my beloved, and his desire is for me."

Discussion Questions:

1. How do you define passion in your marriage, and what role does it play in your relationship?

2. Share personal experiences of moments when you felt deeply passionate about each other.

3. What steps can you take to reignite and sustain passion in your marriage?

Activities:

1. Plan a romantic getaway or weekend escape to reconnect and spend quality time together.

2. Share your fantasies, desires, and aspirations, creating an atmosphere of trust and openness in your relationship.

3. Commit to creating a physical connection every day – holding hands, hugging, whatever provides the connection you need.

Week 14: A Prayer for Financial Wisdom and Unity

F inances can be a significant source of stress in marriages, but they can also be an opportunity for growth, trust, and unity. In Week 14, we will focus on praying for financial wisdom and unity in managing your finances as a couple.

Prayer Prompt:

Heavenly Father,

We come before you seeking your guidance and wisdom in managing our finances. Help us to be good stewards of the resources you have blessed us with. May our financial decisions be aligned with your will, and may we find unity and harmony in our financial journey. In Jesus' name, we pray. Amen.

Scripture Reflection:

- Proverbs 3:9-10 (NIV)
  "Honor the Lord with your wealth, with the first fruits of all your crops; then your barns will be filled to overflowing, and your vats will brim over with new wine."

Discussion Questions:

1. How do you currently approach financial matters in your marriage, and what are your individual financial values and goals?

2. Share any financial challenges or disagreements you've faced in the past. How did you resolve them, and what did you learn from those experiences?

3. How can you apply the principles of Proverbs 3:9-10 to your financial decisions and practices as a couple?

Activities:

1. Set aside time to discuss your shared financial goals and priorities.

2. Explore resources on financial management and consider attending a financial workshop or seeking advice from a financial advisor.

3. Start a financial journal to track your spending habits and financial progress as a couple.

Week 15: Biblical Principles for Financial Stewardship

G od's Word offers valuable insights into how we should manage our finances as Christians. In Week 15, we will explore these biblical principles and apply them to your financial stewardship as a couple.

Prayer Prompt:

Dear Lord,

Thank you for providing us with the guidance we need to manage our finances according to your will. Open our hearts and minds to the biblical principles of stewardship, generosity, and contentment. May our financial decisions reflect our trust in you and our commitment to your kingdom. In Jesus' name, we pray. Amen.

Scripture Reflection:

- Malachi 3:10 (NIV)

  "Bring the whole tithe into the storehouse, that there may be food in my house. Test me in this," says the Lord Almighty, "and see if I will not throw open the floodgates of heaven and pour out so much blessing that there will not be room enough to store it."

Discussion Questions:

1. What biblical principles related to finances resonate with you, and why?

2. How can you integrate the concept of tithing and generosity into your financial plan as a couple?

3. In what ways can you foster contentment and gratitude in your financial journey?

Activities:

1. Commit to tithing or increasing your giving to a charitable cause or your local church, and discuss the impact of your generosity.

2. Study biblical stories of financial stewardship, such as the parable of the talents, and reflect on the lessons they offer.

3. Identify areas where you can simplify your lifestyle and practice contentment in your financial choices.

Week 16: Budgeting and Financial Planning

C reating a budget and financial plan is a practical step toward financial stability and peace in marriage. In Week 16, we will focus on praying for the development of a budget and a financial plan that aligns with your shared goals and values.

Prayer Prompt:

Gracious Father,

Guide us as we embark on the journey of budgeting and financial planning. May our budget reflect our priorities and values as a couple, and may our financial plan bring us closer to our goals. Grant us the discipline and wisdom to manage our resources responsibly. In Jesus' name, we pray. Amen.

Scripture Reflection:

- Proverbs 21:5 (NIV)
  "The plans of the diligent lead to profit as surely as haste leads to poverty."

Discussion Questions:

1. How comfortable are you with the idea of creating a budget and financial plan? What are your initial thoughts and concerns?

2. What are your short-term and long-term financial goals as a couple, and how can a budget help you achieve them?

3. How can you apply the principles of Proverbs 21:5 to your financial planning process?

Activities:

1. Collaboratively create a detailed budget that includes income, expenses, savings, and debt reduction goals.

2. Set a regular time for financial check-ins to track your progress and make adjustments to your budget as needed.

3. Consider seeking financial counseling or attending a financial planning seminar to further enhance your financial knowledge and skills.

Week 17: Financial Communication and Transparency

O pen and honest communication about finances is crucial for building trust and unity in marriage. In Week 17, we will focus on praying for improved financial communication and transparency between you and your spouse.

Prayer Prompt:

Dear Lord,

We recognize the importance of transparent communication in our financial matters. Help us to be open, honest, and understanding when discussing money. May our financial conversations lead to greater unity and trust in our marriage. In Jesus' name, we pray. Amen.

Scripture Reflection:

- Proverbs 22:7 (NIV)
  "The rich rule over the poor, and the borrower is slave to the lender."

Discussion Questions:

1. How comfortable are you with discussing financial matters with your spouse? What barriers or challenges have you faced in the past?

2. Share your individual financial backgrounds, including your upbringing and any financial beliefs or habits you inherited.

3. How can you improve financial communication and transparency in your relationship?

Activities:

1. Schedule regular financial meetings where you discuss your financial goals, progress, and concerns openly and honestly.

2. Share your financial dreams and aspirations, and identify common goals to work toward.

3. Create a financial vision board or chart to visualize your shared financial goals and track your progress together.

Week 18: A Prayer for Family Unity and Parenting Wisdom

F amily is the cornerstone of society, and within a Christian marriage, the family unit is a sacred gift from God. In Week 18, we will focus on praying for family unity and seeking parenting wisdom as you navigate the joys and challenges of raising a family.

Prayer Prompt:

Heavenly Father,

We come before you as a family, seeking your guidance and wisdom in nurturing our family's unity. Strengthen our bonds with love and understanding. Grant us the wisdom and grace to parent our children according to your will. May our family be a reflection of your love and teachings. In Jesus' name, we pray. Amen.

Scripture Reflection:

- Psalm 133:1 (NIV)
  "How good and pleasant it is when God's people live together in unity!"

Discussion Questions:

1. How do you envision your family's unity and the role you play in nurturing it?

2. Share your parenting philosophies and values. In what ways do they align with your Christian faith?

3. What are some challenges you've faced as parents, and how can you seek God's wisdom and guidance to overcome them?

Activities:

1. Dedicate time each day for family devotions, prayer, or reading Scripture together to strengthen your spiritual unity.

2. Create a family mission statement that outlines your shared values and goals as a family.

3. Read books on Christian parenting and discuss how you can incorporate biblical principles into your parenting approach.

Week 19: Biblical Guidance on Parenting

The Bible provides valuable guidance on parenting, offering insights on discipline, love, and the responsibility of raising children in the ways of the Lord. In Week 19, we will explore these biblical principles and apply them to your parenting journey.

Prayer Prompt:

Dear Lord,

We seek your wisdom and guidance as we delve into the biblical teachings on parenting. Help us to be parents who lead our children in your ways, teaching them love, compassion, and faith. May our parenting be a reflection of your grace and wisdom. In Jesus' name, we pray. Amen.

Scripture Reflection:

- Proverbs 22:6 (NIV)
  "Start children off on the way they should go, and even when they are old, they will not turn from it."

Discussion Questions:

1. What are your personal beliefs and values regarding parenting, and how do they align with your Christian faith?

2. Share any parenting challenges or concerns you have encountered. How can you apply biblical principles to address them?

3. How can you implement the wisdom found in Proverbs 22:6 in your parenting journey?

Activities:

1. Identify specific biblical passages that provide parenting guidance and reflect on their relevance to your family's situation.

2. Discuss discipline methods that align with your Christian values and beliefs.

3. Develop a family Bible study routine or prayer time with your children to foster their spiritual growth.

Week 20: Parenting Challenges and Solutions

P arenting is a journey filled with joys, triumphs, and challenges. In Week 20, we will focus on praying for strength and seeking practical solutions to address common parenting challenges that couples often face.

Prayer Prompt:

Gracious Father,

We acknowledge that parenting comes with its unique challenges. Grant us the strength to face these challenges with grace, love, and patience. May we find practical solutions and support one another as we navigate the complexities of parenting. In Jesus' name, we pray. Amen.

Scripture Reflection:

- Philippians 4:13 (NIV)
  "I can do all this through him who gives me strength."

Discussion Questions:

1. What are some of the most significant parenting challenges you've encountered as a couple?

2. Share any experiences where you successfully addressed a parenting challenge together. What strategies or solutions did you find effective?

3. How can you apply the message of Philippians 4:13 to your approach to parenting challenges?

Activities:

1. Create a list of your top parenting challenges and brainstorm potential solutions together.

2. Seek advice and support from other parents within your Christian community or through parenting groups.

3. Dedicate time to discuss and implement positive parenting strategies that align with your Christian values.

Week 21: Teaching Faith and Values to Your Children

As Christian parents, one of your primary responsibilities is to nurture your children's faith and instill godly values in them. In Week 21, we will focus on praying for the wisdom and guidance to effectively teach faith and values to your children.

Prayer Prompt:

Heavenly Father,

We thank you for entrusting us with the responsibility of teaching our children about faith and values. May our words and actions reflect your love and teachings. Grant us the wisdom and patience to guide our children in the ways of the Lord. In Jesus' name, we pray. Amen.

Scripture Reflection:

- Deuteronomy 6:6-7 (NIV)
  "These commandments that I give you today are to be on your hearts. Impress them on your children. Talk about them when you sit at home and when you walk along the road, when you lie down and when you get up."

Discussion Questions:

1. How do you envision teaching your children about faith and values within your Christian marriage?

2. Share examples of how you have already begun teaching your children about God and His teachings.

3. What strategies and approaches can you implement to consistently impart faith and values to your children, as suggested by Deuteronomy 6:6-7?

Activities:

1. Teach your children during family Bible study time, incorporating age-appropriate materials for your children.

2. Encourage your children to ask questions about faith and engage in open, honest, and age-appropriate discussions.

3. Engage in acts of service and volunteer work as a family to instill values of compassion and helping others in need.

Week 22: A Prayer for Resolving Conflicts in a Godly Manner

Conflict is a natural part of any relationship, including marriage. In Week 22, we will focus on praying for the wisdom and grace to resolve conflicts in a godly and constructive manner, strengthening your relationship in the process.

Prayer Prompt:

Gracious Father,

We come before you seeking your guidance and wisdom in resolving conflicts within our marriage. Help us to approach disagreements with love, patience, and humility. May our conflicts lead to growth and understanding, and may our unity be restored through your grace. In Jesus' name, we pray. Amen.

Scripture Reflection:

- Ephesians 4:32 (NIV)
  "Be kind and compassionate to one another, forgiving each other, just as in Christ God forgave you."

Discussion Questions:

1. How do you currently handle conflicts within your marriage, and what emotions do conflicts typically evoke in both of you?

2. Share a past conflict that led to positive growth or understanding within your relationship. What contributed to the resolution of that conflict?

3. How can you apply the teachings of Ephesians 4:32 to your approach to conflict resolution in your marriage?

Activities:

1. Create a conflict resolution plan or strategy together, outlining steps for addressing conflicts in a healthy and constructive way.

2. Practice active listening skills and empathy by taking turns sharing your perspectives during disagreements.

3. Read books or attend workshops on conflict resolution and communication within marriage to enhance your skills.

Week 23: Biblical Insights on Conflict Resolution

T he Bible offers valuable insights on resolving conflicts and pro-
moting reconciliation. In Week 23, we will explore these biblical
principles and apply them to your approach to conflict resolution within
your marriage.

Prayer Prompt:

Dear Lord,

We seek your wisdom and guidance as we explore the biblical teachings
on conflict resolution. Help us to embody the principles of forgiveness, reconciliation, and love as we navigate conflicts in our marriage.
May our conflicts draw us closer to each other and you. In Jesus' name,
we pray. Amen.

Scripture Reflection:

- Matthew 5:23-24 (NIV)
  "Therefore, if you are offering your gift at the altar and there remember that your brother or sister has something against you, leave your gift there in front of the altar. First go and be reconciled to them; then come and offer your gift."

Discussion Questions:

1. Share your understanding of biblical principles related to conflict resolution, such as forgiveness and reconciliation.

2. Reflect on a time when you sought reconciliation with someone who had an issue with you. What did you learn from that experience?

3. How can you apply the message of Matthew 5:23-24 to your approach to resolving conflicts within your marriage?

Activities:

1. Memorize and meditate on key Bible verses related to conflict resolution and forgiveness.

2. Create a list of actionable steps for seeking reconciliation and forgiveness when conflicts arise.

3. Consider reaching out to a Christian counselor or pastor for guidance on implementing biblical conflict resolution principles in your marriage.

Week 24: Conflict Resolution Exercises and Role-Plays

P ractical exercises and role-plays can help you and your spouse develop essential conflict-resolution skills. In Week 24, we will engage in activities to strengthen your ability to navigate conflicts effectively.

Prayer Prompt:

Heavenly Father,

As we engage in practical exercises and role-plays to enhance our conflict-resolution skills, we ask for your guidance and wisdom. May these activities help us become more effective communicators and reconcilers in our marriage. In Jesus' name, we pray. Amen.

Scripture Reflection:

- James 1:19-20 (NIV)
  "My dear brothers and sisters, take note of this: Everyone should be quick to listen, slow to speak and slow to become angry, because human anger does not produce the righteousness that God desires."

Discussion Questions:

1. How do you feel about engaging in conflict-resolution exercises and role-plays as a couple?

2. Reflect on any past experiences where role-playing or practical exercises helped you improve your communication or conflict-resolution skills.

3. How can you apply the wisdom found in James 1:19-20 to your approach to conflict resolution activities?

Activities:

1. Practice active listening and empathetic responses through reverse role-play scenarios based on common conflicts you face as a couple. Make a list of scenarios of previous conflicts then role-play as the other person to gain their perspective of the situation.

2. Create a safe space for open and honest discussions by setting aside time for conflict resolution exercises and opening that time with a prayer together.

3. Explore resources and books that provide practical exercises for enhancing communication and conflict resolution within marriage.

Week 25: Serving Together

Serving others as a couple not only strengthens your bond but also aligns with the teachings of Jesus. In Week 25, we will focus on praying for opportunities to serve together and make a positive impact on your community.

Prayer Prompt:

Dear Lord,

We thank you for the opportunity to serve others as a couple. May our acts of service reflect your love and compassion for those in need. Bless our efforts to make a positive impact on our community and strengthen our relationship as we serve together. In Jesus' name, we pray. Amen.

Scripture Reflection:

- Galatians 5:13 (NIV)

   "You, my brothers and sisters, were called to be free. But do not use your freedom to indulge the flesh; rather, serve one another humbly in love."

Discussion Questions:

1. How do you view the role of serving others within your marriage and as an expression of your Christian faith?

2. Share any past experiences of serving together as a couple. What impact did it have on your relationship and your community?

3. How can you apply the message of Galatians 5:13 to your commitment to serve others humbly in love?

Activities:

1. Identify local volunteer opportunities or charitable organizations that align with your interests and values, and commit to serving together regularly.

2. Create a family mission statement that includes a commitment to service as a core value.

3. Document your service experiences and the impact they have on your community, creating a scrapbook or journal to commemorate your journey of service together.

Week 26: Finding Joy in Serving Together

Week 26 centers around the theme of finding joy together in unity as a Christian couple. Serving others is a beautiful expression of your faith and love for one another. This week, you will explore the importance of unity in your service efforts and how it can strengthen both your marriage and your impact on the world.

Prayer Prompt:

Heavenly Father,

As we embark on a week of serving together in unity, we ask for your guidance and grace. Help us to find harmony in our service endeavors and to be a source of love and hope to those we serve. In Jesus' name, we pray. Amen.

Scripture Reflection:

- Philippians 2:2-4 (NIV)
  "Then make my joy complete by being like-minded, having the same love, being one in spirit and of one mind. Do nothing out of selfish ambition or vain conceit. Rather, in humility value others above yourselves, not looking to your own interests but each of you to the interests of the others."

Discussion Questions:

1. Reflect on your past experiences serving together as a couple. How has unity played a role in the joy you experience in service?

2. Share your individual strengths and talents when it comes to serving others. How can you leverage these strengths to create unity in your service projects?

3. How can you apply the message of Philippians 2:2-4, emphasizing unity in love and humility in service, to your commitment to serve together as a harmonious couple?

Activities:

1. Celebrate each other by creating a culture of appreciation for your partner's service to others.

2. Create a joint mission statement outlining your commitment to serving in unity and the positive impact you hope to make in your community.

3. Dedicate time to discuss the ways you can foster unity within your marriage and service endeavors, emphasizing humility and selflessness.

Week 27: The Impact of Serving Together

Week 27 explores the impact of serving together as a couple on your marriage, faith, and the lives of those you serve. Engaging in acts of service can deepen your connection, strengthen your sense of purpose, and bring you closer to God. This week, you will reflect on the significance of your service journey.

Prayer Prompt:

Dear Lord,

As we reflect on the impact of serving together, we thank you for the opportunities to make a difference in the lives of others. May our acts of service continue to strengthen our marriage, deepen our faith, and bring us closer to you. In Jesus' name, we pray. Amen.

Scripture Reflection:

- 1 Peter 4:10 (NIV)
  "Each of you should use whatever gift you have received to serve others, as faithful stewards of God's grace in its various forms."

Discussion Questions:

1. Reflect on the acts of service you've undertaken as a couple. How have these experiences impacted your relationship, faith, and perspective on the world?

2. Share any personal stories or moments of inspiration that arose from your service journey together.

3. How can you apply the message of 1 Peter 4:10, emphasizing using your gifts to serve others as stewards of God's grace, to your commitment to continue serving together?

Activities:

1. Create a scrapbook or journal that documents your service journey, including photos, reflections, and the people you've met along the way.

2. Dedicate time to discuss the impact of your service experiences on your marriage, and set new service goals for the future.

3. Plan a joint service project or fundraiser to support a cause you are both passionate about, and invite friends and family to join in

your mission.

Week 28: A Prayer of Thanksgiving for Your Marriage

In Week 28, we pause to express our gratitude to God for the gift of your marriage. We reflect on the journey you've undertaken and the blessings you've experienced along the way.

Prayer Prompt:

Gracious Father,

We come before you with hearts filled with gratitude for the precious gift of our marriage. Thank you for the love, companionship, and shared experiences we have enjoyed. As we reflect on our journey, may our hearts be filled with thanksgiving for your faithfulness and grace. In Jesus' name, we pray. Amen.

Scripture Reflection:

- Psalm 136:26 (NIV)
  "Give thanks to the God of heaven. His love endures forever."

Discussion Questions:

1. Reflect on your marriage journey. What are some of the most cherished moments and blessings you've experienced together?

2. How has your faith and your relationship with God evolved since you began this year of prayer for your marriage?

3. In what ways can you continue to cultivate a spirit of thanksgiving and gratitude within your marriage?

Activities:

1. Write individual letters of gratitude to each other, expressing your appreciation for specific qualities and moments in your marriage.

2. Create a list of milestones and achievements you've celebrated as a couple and display it prominently in your home.

3. Dedicate time to pray together, thanking God for your marriage and the journey you've shared.

Week 29: Celebrating Your Love Story

E very marriage has a unique and beautiful love story. In Week 29, we will focus on celebrating your love story, from the moment you met to the present day, and all the special moments in between.

Prayer Prompt:

Heavenly Father,

We thank you for the love story you've written for us. As we celebrate our journey, we are reminded of your divine plan and the way our paths intertwine. Bless our love story and continue to fill it with joy, purpose, and significance. In Jesus' name, we pray. Amen.

Scripture Reflection:

- Song of Solomon 8:7 (NIV)
  "Many waters cannot quench love; rivers cannot sweep it away."

Discussion Questions:

1. Share the story of how you met and fell in love. What were the defining moments that brought you together?

2. Reflect on the growth and transformation you've experienced as a couple since the beginning of your journey.

3. How can you keep your love story alive and vibrant, even as you continue to grow and change together?

Activities:

1. Create a timeline of your love story, including key moments, milestones, and memorable experiences.

2. Celebrate your love with a special date night or romantic getaway dedicated to reminiscing about your journey.

3. Write down your hopes and dreams for the future of your love story and the legacy you want to leave together.

Week 30: Celebrating Each Other's Uniqueness

Week 30 focuses on the importance of celebrating each other's uniqueness within your marriage. Each individual brings their own strengths, talents, and quirks to the relationship. Embracing and honoring these differences can deepen your love and connection as a couple.

Prayer Prompt:

Gracious Father,

As we delve into the significance of celebrating each other's uniqueness, we seek your guidance. Help us appreciate and cherish the individuality that each of us brings to our marriage. May our love grow stronger as we honor and celebrate our differences. In Jesus' name, we pray. Amen.

Scripture Reflection:

- Psalm 139:13-14 (NIV)

  "For you created my inmost being; you knit me together in my mother's womb. I praise you because I am fearfully and wonderfully made; your works are wonderful, I know that full well."

Discussion Questions:

1. Reflect on the unique qualities and strengths that each of you brings to the marriage. How have these differences enriched your relationship?

2. Share moments when you've celebrated each other's uniqueness and the positive impact it had on your connection.

3. How can you apply the message of Psalm 139:13-14, emphasizing God's wonderful and intentional creation, to your commitment to celebrating each other's uniqueness?

Activities:

1. Create a list of each other's unique qualities, talents, and quirks that you appreciate and celebrate.

2. Plan a surprise date night or special activity that incorporates each other's interests or hobbies, celebrating your individuality.

3. Dedicate time to write heartfelt letters or notes to each other, expressing your love and appreciation for the unique qualities that

make your partner special.

Week 31: Celebrating Your Journey Together

In Week 31, we will celebrate the journey you've undertaken as a couple. This is a time to reflect on your shared experiences, growth, and the adventures that lie ahead.

Prayer Prompt:

Gracious Father,

As we celebrate our journey together, we thank you for the adventures, challenges, and growth we've experienced. Bless our future as a couple, and may our journey continue to be marked by love, faith, and unity. In Jesus' name, we pray. Amen.

Scripture Reflection:

- Proverbs 16:9 (NIV)
  "In their hearts humans plan their course, but the Lord establishes their steps."

Discussion Questions:

1. Reflect on the adventures and milestones you've experienced as a couple. What are some of the most memorable moments of your journey together?

2. Share your hopes and dreams for the future of your marriage. How can you continue to grow and strengthen your bond in the years to come?

3. How can you embrace the idea that God is the ultimate author of your journey, as suggested by Proverbs 16:9?

Activities:

1. Create a "journey board" or collage with photos and mementos from your adventures together, displaying it prominently in your home.

2. Plan a special date or getaway to celebrate your journey, focusing on creating new memories and experiences.

3. Reflect on the lessons and insights you've gained from your journey and discuss how they have shaped your marriage and faith.

Week 32: Nurturing Your Spiritual Growth

Week 32 is dedicated to nurturing your spiritual growth both individually and as a couple. Just as plants require care and nourishment to flourish, your spiritual lives need intentional attention and nurturing to thrive. This week, you will explore ways to deepen your connection with God and with each other through spiritual growth.

Prayer Prompt:

Heavenly Father,

As we focus on nurturing our spiritual growth, we seek your wisdom and guidance. May our hearts be open to your word, and may our faith flourish. Help us grow closer to you and each other as we journey together. In Jesus' name, we pray. Amen.

Scripture Reflection:

- Psalm 1:3 (NIV)
  "That person is like a tree planted by streams of water, which yields its fruit in season and whose leaf does not wither—whatever they do prospers."

Discussion Questions:

1. Reflect on your individual spiritual journeys and the growth you've experienced. How can you nurture your spiritual growth as a couple?

2. Share specific spiritual practices or rituals that have been meaningful to you individually and discuss how you can incorporate them as a couple.

3. How can you apply the message of Psalm 1:3, emphasizing the prospering of a well-nourished tree, to your commitment to nurturing your spiritual growth together?

Activities:

1. Set aside dedicated time for joint Bible study or devotional reading, selecting a passage or topic that resonates with both of you.

2. Create a prayer journal or gratitude journal together, where you record your prayers, reflections, and spiritual insights.

3. Plan a visit to a local church, spiritual retreat, or event that aligns

with your spiritual growth goals and provides an opportunity for
learning and reflection.

Week 33: Aligning Your Spiritual Goals

Week 33 explores the importance of aligning your spiritual goals as a couple. Just as a compass points toward true north, aligning your spiritual journey can help you navigate life's challenges and blessings together. This week, you will reflect on your shared spiritual goals and how they can strengthen your marriage.

Prayer Prompt:

Dear Lord,

As we delve into the idea of aligning our spiritual goals, we invite your presence into our marriage. Guide us in setting and pursuing goals that deepen our faith and connection with you. May our spiritual alignment be a source of unity and purpose. In Jesus' name, we pray. Amen.

Scripture Reflection:

- Amos 3:3 (NIV)
  "Do two walk together unless they have agreed to do so?"

Discussion Questions:

1. Reflect on your shared spiritual goals and aspirations. How do they contribute to your marriage and faith journey?

2. Share specific ways you can support each other in achieving these goals and discuss the steps you'll take to align your spiritual paths.

3. How can you apply the message of Amos 3:3, emphasizing the importance of agreement and alignment, to your commitment to aligning your spiritual goals as a couple?

Activities:

1. Make individual lists of passages that best describe your spiritual goals; share these and discuss how they make you feel.

2. Dedicate a joint journal or digital document to document your progress toward your shared spiritual goals and the insights you gain along the way.

3. Plan a getaway or retreat focused on aligning your spiritual journeys, where you can engage in meaningful discussions and activities to deepen your connection with God and each other.

Week 34: A Prayer for the Future of Your Marriage

It's time to look ahead and seek God's guidance for the future of your marriage. In Week 34, we will focus on praying for His blessings, direction, and grace as you continue your journey together.

Prayer Prompt:

Dear Lord,

As we look to the future of our marriage, we place it in your hands. Guide us, protect us, and bless us as we move forward. May our commitment to each other and you remain unwavering, and may our love continue to grow. In Jesus' name, we pray. Amen.

Scripture Reflection:

- Jeremiah 29:11 (NIV)
  "For I know the plans I have for you," declares the Lord, "plans to prosper you and not to harm you, plans to give you hope and a future."

Discussion Questions:

1. What hopes and dreams do you have for the future of your marriage, both individually and as a couple?

2. Reflect on the lessons you've learned and the growth you've experienced throughout this year of prayer. How can you apply these lessons to your future together?

3. How can you trust in God's plans and seek His guidance for the future, as emphasized in Jeremiah 29:11?

Activities:

1. Discuss your individual roles and responsibilities in achieving your future goals and how they align with your faith.

2. Set aside time to tell each other the qualities you admire in each other and how they will contribute to building your future together.

3. Dedicate time for a special prayer session, where you both pray for God's guidance and blessings on your future as a couple.

Week 35: Setting New Goals and Dreams

In Week 35, you will have the opportunity to set new goals and dreams as a couple. As you look ahead, it's essential to define your shared vision and purpose.

Prayer Prompt:

Heavenly Father,

As we set new goals and dreams for our marriage, we invite your wisdom and guidance. Help us to align our desires with your will and to pursue a future that glorifies you. May our shared vision be a testament to your love and grace. In Jesus' name, we pray. Amen.

Scripture Reflection:

- Proverbs 16:3 (NIV)

  "Commit to the Lord whatever you do, and he will establish your plans."

Discussion Questions:

1. What new goals and dreams do you want to set for your marriage? How do they align with your faith and values?

2. Share the steps and strategies you plan to implement to achieve these goals and dreams.

3. How can you commit your plans to the Lord and trust in His guidance, as emphasized in Proverbs 16:3?

Activities:

1. Create a list of short-term and long-term goals for your marriage and establish a timeline for achieving them.

2. Set aside time for a joint vision board activity where you visualize your shared dreams and aspirations.

3. Begin a journal where you document your progress toward your goals and reflect on the role of faith in your journey.

Week 36: Aligning Your Life Goals

Week 36 focuses on the importance of aligning your life goals as a couple. Just as stars in the night sky align to create constellations, aligning your goals can help you navigate life's journey together and strengthen your marriage. This week, you will explore the process of aligning your life goals and how it can lead to a more harmonious and purposeful partnership.

Prayer Prompt:

Heavenly Father,

As we delve into the idea of aligning our life goals, we seek your guidance and wisdom. Help us to set and pursue goals that bring us closer together and honor your plans for our lives. May our alignment lead to a more purposeful and loving marriage. In Jesus' name, we pray. Amen.

Scripture Reflection:

- Proverbs 19:21 (NIV)
  "Many are the plans in a person's heart, but it is the Lord's purpose that prevails."

Discussion Questions:

1. Reflect on your individual life goals and aspirations. How can you align these goals to create a shared vision for your future as a couple?

2. Share specific steps you can take to support each other in achieving your aligned life goals and discuss any potential challenges you may face.

3. How can you apply the message of Proverbs 19:21, emphasizing the Lord's purpose prevailing, to your commitment to aligning your life goals as a couple?

Activities:

1. Make a plan for semi-annual check-ins to discuss your goals.

2. Set aside dedicated time to create a joint mission statement outlining your commitment to aligning your life goals and the positive impact you hope to make together.

3. Plan a future-focused date night or weekend getaway where you both discuss your aligned life goals and take practical steps toward

achieving them.

Week 37: Committing to a Lifetime of Prayer

Recognize that prayer is an ongoing and vital part of your marriage. In Week 37, you will commit to continue praying together for a lifetime.

Prayer Prompt:

Gracious Father,

We commit to a lifetime of seeking your presence and guidance through prayer. May our faith and love for you and each other grow stronger with each passing day. Bless our marriage with the gift of prayer, and may it be a source of strength, unity, and joy. In Jesus' name, we pray. Amen.

Scripture Reflection:

- 1 Thessalonians 5:16-18 (NIV)
  "Rejoice always, pray continually, give thanks in all circumstances; for this is God's will for you in Christ Jesus."

Discussion Questions:

1. How do you envision the role of prayer within your marriage in the years to come?

2. Share specific commitments you are willing to make to ensure that prayer remains a central part of your relationship.

3. How can you incorporate the teachings of 1 Thessalonians 5:16-18 into your daily lives and commitment to prayer?

Activities:

1. Write a prayer commitment statement together, outlining your shared commitment to a lifetime of prayer in your marriage.

2. Establish a regular prayer routine that includes daily or weekly prayer sessions as a couple.

3. Consider joining a couples' prayer group or seeking mentorship from a more experienced Christian couple to support and strengthen your prayer life.

Week 38: Finding Peace Together in Prayer

I n Week 38, you will embrace praying together as a couple. It's a time to speak together, seek God's blessings for your future, and acknowledge the transformation that prayer has brought to your marriage.

Prayer Prompt:

Dear Lord,

We thank you for your faithfulness and presence in our marriage. Bless our future as a couple, and may our love and faith continue to grow. We entrust our journey to you, seeking your guidance and grace. In Jesus' name, we pray. Amen.

Scripture Reflection:

- Numbers 6:24-26 (NIV)
  "The Lord bless you and keep you; the Lord make his face shine on you and be gracious to you; the Lord turn his face toward you and give you peace."

Discussion Questions:

1. Reflect on the impact praying together has on your marriage and faith. How has it transformed your relationship and your individual spiritual journeys?

2. Share your hopes and aspirations for the future of your marriage, and how prayer will continue to play a central role.

3. How can you apply the blessing from Numbers 6:24-26 to your marriage and your commitment to a future filled with God's grace and peace?

Activities:

1. Create a family prayer that you can always return to when you need to regain peace and harmony in your lives.

2. Continue to add to your journal that documents your year of praying together, capturing the highlights and reflections.

3. Dedicate time for a prayer session, where you both express your gratitude, hopes, and commitment to prayer in your marriage

moving forward.

Week 39: Cultivating Gratitude in Your Marriage

Week 39 is dedicated to the practice of cultivating gratitude in your marriage. Gratitude is a powerful force that can deepen your connection, foster contentment, and strengthen your relationship with God. This week, you will explore the significance of gratitude and how to incorporate it into your marriage.

Prayer Prompt:

Gracious Father,

As we focus on cultivating gratitude, we seek your presence and guidance. Open our hearts to the blessings in our lives, and help us express our gratitude to each other and you. May our marriage be filled with thankfulness and love. In Jesus' name, we pray. Amen.

Scripture Reflection:

- 1 Thessalonians 5:18 (NIV)
  "Give thanks in all circumstances; for this is God's will for you in Christ Jesus."

Discussion Questions:

1. Reflect on the role of gratitude in your marriage. How have expressions of gratitude impacted your relationship and connection?

2. Share specific moments or experiences when you felt grateful for your spouse. How can you continue to cultivate gratitude in your daily lives?

3. How can you apply the message of 1 Thessalonians 5:18, emphasizing giving thanks in all circumstances, to your commitment to cultivating gratitude in your marriage?

Activities:

1. Begin a gratitude journal or notebook where you both regularly write down things you appreciate about each other and the blessings in your lives.

2. Plan a gratitude-focused date night or evening where you take turns expressing your gratitude for specific aspects of your marriage.

3. Dedicate time for a joint prayer of gratitude, thanking God for each other and the love you share.

Week 40: Finding Contentment in Your Marriage

Week 40 centers on the theme of finding contentment in your marriage. Contentment is a valuable virtue that can lead to a more joyful and peaceful relationship. This week, you will explore the concept of contentment and its significance in building a strong and lasting marriage.

Prayer Prompt:

Dear Lord,

As we delve into the idea of finding contentment, we invite your presence into our hearts and marriage. Help us to find peace and satisfaction in our relationship, knowing that you are the source of our true contentment. In Jesus' name, we pray. Amen.

Scripture Reflection:

- Philippians 4:11-12 (NIV)
  "I have learned to be content whatever the circumstances. I know what it is to be in need, and I know what it is to have plenty. I have learned the secret of being content in any and every situation, whether well fed or hungry, whether living in plenty or in want."

Discussion Questions:

1. Reflect on the concept of contentment in your marriage. How has contentment played a role in your happiness and fulfillment as a couple?

2. Share moments when you've felt content in your relationship. How can you continue to nurture and maintain this sense of contentment?

3. How can you apply the message of Philippians 4:11-12, emphasizing learning to be content in all circumstances, to your commitment to finding contentment in your marriage?

Activities:

1. Create a list of the things that bring you contentment in your marriage and regularly revisit and update it together.

2. Dedicate time for a peaceful and contentment-focused date night, where you engage in relaxing activities that bring you joy and satisfaction.

3. Discuss and set mutual goals for finding contentment in your marriage, emphasizing the importance of appreciating the present moment and cherishing each other.

Week 41: Embracing Continued Growth

Week 41 is dedicated to embracing continual growth in your marriage and faith journey. Just as a tree grows and bears fruit over time, your marriage and spiritual life have the potential for ongoing development and enrichment. This week, you will reflect on the progress you've made and set intentions for continued growth.

Prayer Prompt:

Heavenly Father,

As we embark on a week of contemplating continued growth, we seek your guidance and blessings. May our marriage and faith journey always be marked by growth and transformation. Help us remain open to your guidance and embrace the path of ongoing development. In Jesus' name, we pray. Amen.

Scripture Reflection:

- 2 Corinthians 3:18 (NIV)
  "And we all, who with unveiled faces contemplate the Lord's glory, are being transformed into his image with ever-increasing glory, which comes from the Lord, who is the Spirit."

Discussion Questions:

1. Reflect on the journey of growth you've experienced as a couple and in your faith. What have been the most significant moments and insights?

2. Share the specific areas of your relationship and faith that you hope to nurture and develop further.

3. How can you apply the message of 2 Corinthians 3:18, emphasizing ongoing transformation into the image of the Lord, to your commitment to a lifetime of growth in your marriage and faith?

Activities:

1. Create a list of goals and aspirations for your marriage and faith, outlining your vision for the future and the steps you'll take to achieve them.

2. Plan a yearly reflection and renewal ceremony where you revisit your commitment and set new goals for your journey together.

3. Dedicate time for a closing prayer session, where you both offer

prayers of commitment and blessing for the ongoing growth of your marriage and faith.

Week 42: Engaging in Community and Fellowship

Week 42 centers on the importance of engaging in community and fellowship as a couple. Being part of a supportive community and seeking fellowship with other believers can enrich your marriage and spiritual journey. This week, you will explore the significance of community and how to actively engage in it.

Prayer Prompt:

Heavenly Father,

As we focus on community and fellowship, we seek your guidance and blessings. Help us to connect with like-minded individuals and deepen our sense of community both within and outside our marriage. May our fellowship bring us closer to you and each other. In Jesus' name, we pray. Amen.

Scripture Reflection:

- Hebrews 10:24-25 (NIV)

  "And let us consider how we may spur one another on toward love and good deeds, not giving up meeting together, as some are in the habit of doing, but encouraging one another—and all the more as you see the Day approaching."

Discussion Questions:

1. Reflect on your current involvement in a community or fellowship group. How has it impacted your marriage and faith?

2. Share any past experiences of fellowship that were particularly meaningful or uplifting. How can you incorporate similar experiences into your life as a couple?

3. How can you apply the message of Hebrews 10:24-25, emphasizing the importance of meeting together and encouraging one another, to your commitment to engaging in community and fellowship?

Activities:

1. Research local churches, small groups, or community organizations that align with your beliefs and interests, and plan to attend a meeting or event together.

2. Create a list of potential ways you can serve or contribute to your chosen community or fellowship group, and discuss your roles

and commitments.

3. Dedicate time for a joint reflection on the impact of community and fellowship on your marriage, and set goals for how you can continue to engage in these meaningful connections.

Week 43: Strengthening Your Fellowship Together

Week 43 delves deeper into the theme of strengthening your fellowship together as a couple. Building and nurturing relationships within your chosen community can bring you closer to God and enhance your sense of belonging. This week, you will explore practical ways to strengthen your fellowship as a couple.

Prayer Prompt:

Dear Lord,

As we focus on strengthening our fellowship, we invite your presence into our hearts and marriage. Help us to build meaningful connections with others and to deepen our sense of belonging. May our fellowship draw us closer to you and to each other. In Jesus' name, we pray. Amen.

Scripture Reflection:

- Acts 2:42 (NIV)
  "They devoted themselves to the apostles' teaching and to fellowship, to the breaking of bread and to prayer."

Discussion Questions:

1. Reflect on your current fellowship experiences and the relationships you've built within your community. How have these connections impacted your faith and marriage?

2. Share your ideas for strengthening your fellowship together as a couple. How can you deepen your involvement and contribute to your chosen community?

3. How can you apply the message of Acts 2:42, emphasizing devotion to fellowship, teaching, and prayer, to your commitment to strengthening your fellowship as a couple?

Activities:

1. Plan a joint visit or outreach activity within your community or fellowship group, where you can actively engage with others and contribute to a shared cause.

2. Set aside designated times for shared prayer or spiritual reflection with friends or community members, deepening your spiritual bonds.

3. Reflect on your own spiritual growth and the impact of fellowship on your marriage, and discuss how you can continue to strengthen your fellowship and contribute to the growth of your chosen community.

Week 44: Reflecting on Your Journey

It's essential to take time to reflect on the journey you've undertaken as a couple. Week 44 provides an opportunity for introspection, celebration, and a renewed commitment to the principles and practices you've explored throughout this book.

Prayer Prompt:

Gracious Father,

As we reflect on the journey we've experienced together, we thank you for your presence and guidance. May our hearts be filled with gratitude for the growth, love, and faith we've cultivated. Bless our continued journey as a couple and our commitment to seeking you in all things. In Jesus' name, we pray. Amen.

Scripture Reflection:

- Psalm 119:105 (NIV)
  "Your word is a lamp for my feet, a light on my path."

Discussion Questions:

1. Reflect on the transformative journey you've undertaken as a couple. What were the most significant moments and insights gained?

2. Share the impact of this year-long experience on your marriage and faith. How have you grown individually and together?

3. How can you apply the message of Psalm 119:105 to your continued commitment to seek God's guidance and light on your path as a couple?

Activities:

1. Create a timeline that showcases key moments and highlights from your journey together, capturing the growth and transformation you've experienced.

2. Write individual letters to each other, expressing your gratitude, love, and reflections on the journey you've shared.

3. Dedicate time for a special closing ceremony where you offer prayers of thanksgiving, commit to your ongoing journey, and celebrate your love and faith.

Week 45: A Renewed Commitment

In Week 45, you will make a renewed commitment to the principles and practices you've explored throughout this book. It's an opportunity to reaffirm your dedication to a strong and faith-filled marriage.

Prayer Prompt:

Dear Lord,

As we conclude this book, we renew our commitment to a strong and faith-filled marriage. May the principles and practices we've embraced continue to guide us, and may our love and faith deepen with each passing day. Bless our marriage, our journey, and our future together. In Jesus' name, we pray. Amen.

Scripture Reflection:

- Colossians 3:14 (NIV)
"And over all these virtues put on love, which binds them all together in perfect unity."

Discussion Questions:

1. Reflect on the commitment you made at the beginning of this book. How have you grown and evolved in your understanding and practice of love, faith, and prayer?

2. Share the aspects of your marriage that you wish to strengthen and nurture in the coming years.

3. How can you apply the message of Colossians 3:14, emphasizing the importance of love binding all virtues together, to your renewed commitment to each other and your faith?

Activities:

1. Create a written or verbal commitment statement, outlining your renewed dedication to love, faith, and prayer in your marriage.

2. Plan a special date night or getaway to celebrate your commitment to each other, focusing on strengthening your bond.

3. Decide on a timeline for a renewal of your commitment; this could be weekly, monthly, or annually – whatever timeline aligns with your goals.

Week 46: Embracing a Lifetime of Growth

Week 46 is a time to embrace the idea that your journey of growth, love, and faith is ongoing. It's an opportunity to recognize that your marriage is a dynamic and evolving partnership, filled with opportunities for continued growth and learning.

Prayer Prompt:

Heavenly Father,

As we embrace the idea of a lifetime of growth in our marriage, we thank you for the journey we've embarked upon. Bless our commitment to learning, growing, and deepening our faith together. May our love be a testament to your grace and guidance. In Jesus' name, we pray. Amen.

Scripture Reflection:

- Philippians 1:6 (NIV)
  "Being confident of this, that he who began a good work in you will carry it on to completion until the day of Christ Jesus."

Discussion Questions:

1. Reflect on the idea that your marriage is a dynamic and evolving partnership. How do you envision your journey of growth in the years to come?

2. Share the specific areas of your relationship and faith that you hope to nurture and develop further.

3. How can you apply the message of Philippians 1:6, trusting that God will continue His good work in you, to your commitment to a lifetime of growth in your marriage?

Activities:

1. Share the commitment statement you created in the previous week with other couples in your community. Use this to start a conversation about growth where you can share and learn from your community.

2. Create a list of ways you can continue to experience growth in the years to come.

3. Dedicate time for a prayer session, where you both offer prayers

of commitment and blessing for the ongoing growth of your marriage and faith.

Week 47: Navigating Sickness Together with Grace

Week 47 is dedicated to the theme of navigating sickness together with grace. Illness and health challenges can be trying times for a marriage, but facing them together can strengthen your bond and demonstrate the depth of your love. This week, you will explore how to support each other during times of sickness.

Prayer Prompt:

Heavenly Father,

As we focus on navigating sickness with grace, we seek your comfort and healing. Be with us during times of illness, and help us to support and care for each other with love and grace. May our marriage remain strong through all challenges. In Jesus' name, we pray. Amen.

Scripture Reflection:

- James 5:14-15 (NIV)

  "Is anyone among you sick? Let them call the elders of the church to pray over them and anoint them with oil in the name of the Lord. And the prayer offered in faith will make the sick person well; the Lord will raise them up."

Discussion Questions:

1. Reflect on any experiences you've had with illness or health challenges in your marriage. How did you support each other during those times?

2. Share your thoughts on how you can better navigate sickness together as a couple, both practically and emotionally.

3. How can you apply the message of James 5:14-15, emphasizing the power of prayer and support during sickness, to your commitment to navigating illness with grace?

Activities:

1. Create a "sickness plan" together, outlining how you will support each other when one of you is unwell, including tasks, communication, and emotional support.

2. Set aside a special time to pray for each other's health and well-being, asking for God's guidance and healing in times of illness.

3. Reflect on past instances when you've cared for each other during illness, and express your gratitude and love for your spouse's support.

Week 48: Celebrating Health and Well-Being Together

Week 48 focuses on celebrating health and well-being together as a couple. In times of good health, it's essential to appreciate the blessings of wellness and to nurture your physical and emotional well-being. This week, you will explore ways to celebrate your health and strengthen your commitment to maintaining it.

Prayer Prompt:

Gracious Father,

As we celebrate health and well-being, we thank you for the gift of vitality and strength. Help us to take care of our bodies and nurture our well-being, so we may continue to serve you and each other. May our marriage be a testament to your goodness. In Jesus' name, we pray. Amen.

Scripture Reflection:

- 1 Corinthians 6:19-20 (NIV)

  "Do you not know that your bodies are temples of the Holy Spirit, who is in you, whom you have received from God? You are not your own; you were bought at a price. Therefore, honor God with your bodies."

Discussion Questions:

1. Reflect on your current health and well-being practices as a couple. How can you better prioritize and celebrate your physical and emotional health?

2. Share your ideas for nurturing your well-being together and discuss any health goals you'd like to set as a couple.

3. How can you apply the message of 1 Corinthians 6:19-20, emphasizing the importance of honoring God with your bodies, to your commitment to celebrating health and well-being together?

Activities:

1. Plan a day of wellness and self-care together, which may include activities like hiking, meditation, a spa day, or preparing a healthy meal together.

2. Create a vision board or list of health and wellness goals as a couple, focusing on both physical and emotional well-being.

3. Dedicate time for a joint prayer of thanksgiving for your health and well-being, expressing gratitude for the strength to serve God and each other.

Week 49: Prioritizing Self-Care Together

Week 49 focuses on the importance of prioritizing self-care together as a couple. Self-care is essential for maintaining physical and emotional well-being, which, in turn, enhances your relationship and allows you to better support each other. This week, you will explore the significance of self-care and how to incorporate it into your marriage.

Prayer Prompt:

Heavenly Father,

As we delve into the theme of self-care, we seek your guidance and wisdom. Help us to prioritize our physical and emotional well-being, so we may continue to serve you and each other with love and strength. May our marriage be a source of rejuvenation and support. In Jesus' name, we pray. Amen.

Scripture Reflection:

- Psalm 23:2-3 (NIV)
  "He makes me lie down in green pastures, he leads me beside quiet waters, he refreshes my soul. He guides me along the right paths for his name's sake."

Discussion Questions:

1. Reflect on your current self-care practices as a couple. How do you prioritize self-care individually and together?

2. Share specific ways you can support each other in self-care, including physical and emotional well-being, and discuss any self-care goals you'd like to set as a couple.

3. How can you apply the message of Psalm 23:2-3, emphasizing the refreshment of the soul and guidance along right paths, to your commitment to prioritizing self-care together?

Activities:

1. Discuss your individual needs for self-care in an open and honest environment.

2. Plan a self-care day or weekend retreat together, where you both engage in activities that rejuvenate and nourish your physical and emotional well-being.

3. Create a self-care calendar or checklist, including regular self-care

activities and dates, and commit to following it as a couple.

Week 50: The Power of Connection

As your journey through this book nears its end, Week 50 focuses on the power of connection in your marriage. Deep and meaningful connections between spouses are essential for maintaining a strong and thriving relationship. This week, you'll explore ways to strengthen your emotional and spiritual connection as a couple.

Prayer Prompt:

Gracious Father,

We thank you for the gift of connection in our marriage. Bless us with the ability to strengthen our emotional and spiritual bonds as we continue our journey together. May our connection be a source of joy, intimacy, and strength. In Jesus' name, we pray. Amen.

Scripture Reflection:

- Ecclesiastes 4:9-10 (NIV)
"Two are better than one, because they have a good return for their labor: If either of them falls down, one can help the other up. But pity anyone who falls and has no one to help them up."

Discussion Questions:

1. Reflect on the importance of emotional and spiritual connection in your marriage. How do you currently nurture these connections?

2. Share specific moments when you felt a deep emotional or spiritual connection with your spouse. What contributed to those moments?

3. How can you apply the message of Ecclesiastes 4:9-10 to your commitment to strengthen your connection as a couple?

Activities:

1. Create a list of activities and practices that help you feel emotionally and spiritually connected, and commit to incorporating them into your daily or weekly routine.

2. Dedicate a date night or special time for deep and meaningful conversation, where you both open up about your thoughts, feelings, and faith.

3. Consider reading a book or attending a workshop on building emotional and spiritual intimacy in marriage.

Week 51: Connecting Through Shared Dreams

Shared dreams and goals can be a powerful source of connection in marriage. In Week 51, you will explore the importance of setting and pursuing shared dreams, and how doing so can strengthen your emotional and spiritual connection as a couple.

Prayer Prompt:

Dear Lord,

As we explore the significance of shared dreams in our marriage, we seek your guidance and wisdom. Bless us with the ability to set and pursue goals that deepen our emotional and spiritual connection. May our dreams be a source of unity and purpose. In Jesus' name, we pray. Amen.

Scripture Reflection:

- Proverbs 16:3 (NIV)

  "Commit to the Lord whatever you do, and he will establish your plans."

Discussion Questions:

1. Reflect on the dreams and goals you have set as a couple. How do they contribute to your emotional and spiritual connection?

2. Share any shared dreams or aspirations that you both have for your marriage and future. What steps can you take to work toward those dreams?

3. How can you apply the message of Proverbs 16:3 to your commitment to setting and pursuing shared dreams?

Activities:

1. Create a word cloud that represents your shared dreams and goals.

2. Set aside time to discuss and refine your shared dreams, outlining actionable steps to bring them closer to reality.

3. Dedicate a joint journal or digital document to document your progress toward your shared dreams and the emotional and spiritual connection you experience throughout the journey.

Week 52: A Lifetime of Connection

As you approach the end of this book, Week 52 is a time to reflect on the importance of a lifetime of connection in your marriage. It's an opportunity to acknowledge that the journey of staying connected is ongoing and that your commitment to emotional and spiritual connection will continue to grow throughout your lives together.

Prayer Prompt:

Heavenly Father,

As we conclude this book, we acknowledge the importance of a lifetime of connection in our marriage. Bless our commitment to staying emotionally and spiritually connected as we grow old together. May our love and faith deepen with each passing day. In Jesus' name, we pray. Amen.

Scripture Reflection:

- 1 Corinthians 13:4-7 (NIV)

  "Love is patient, love is kind. It does not envy, it does not boast, it is not proud. It does not dishonor others, it is not self-seeking, it is not easily angered, it keeps no record of wrongs. Love does not delight in evil but rejoices with the truth. It always protects, always trusts, always hopes, always perseveres."

Discussion Questions:

1. Reflect on the idea of a lifetime of connection in your marriage. How do you envision your emotional and spiritual connection evolving over the years?

2. Share the qualities and practices that have allowed you to stay connected as a couple, and discuss how you plan to nurture them in the future.

3. How can you apply the message of 1 Corinthians 13:4-7, emphasizing love's enduring and selfless nature, to your commitment to a lifetime of emotional and spiritual connection?

Activities:

1. Write a letter or note to each other, expressing your commitment to a lifetime of connection and your hopes for the future.

2. Create a legacy project or family tradition that symbolizes your commitment to emotional and spiritual connection, passing it

down to future generations.

3. Dedicate time for a closing ceremony where you both offer prayers of blessing and thanksgiving for the ongoing growth of your emotional and spiritual connection in your marriage.

Conclusion

With the conclusion of this book, you have embarked on a year-long journey to strengthen your emotional and spiritual connection as a couple. May your commitment to connection continue to deepen your love and faith, allowing your marriage to thrive throughout the years to come. Blessings on your ongoing journey of connection.

As you reach the conclusion of *Growing Together in Faith* we hope that this journey has deepened your bond as a couple, enriched your faith, and fortified your commitment to a lifetime of love, prayer, and partnership.

Throughout the past 52 weeks, you have explored various aspects of your marriage and faith, from communication and intimacy to gratitude, community, and self-care. Your dedication to nurturing your relationship and spiritual growth as a couple is a testament to your love for each other and your shared devotion to God.

Remember that your marriage is a divine gift, a covenant between you, your partner, and the Creator. Just as you have prayed together through the ups and downs, joys and challenges, you have allowed God's presence to dwell at the heart of your relationship.

As you continue your journey together, may your commitment to prayer remain unwavering, your love for each other continue to deepen, and your faith in God's guidance and grace sustain you in all circumstances. May your marriage serve as a beacon of love and hope to others, and may your union be a source of strength and inspiration to all who witness it.

Though this book may conclude, your love story and spiritual journey as a couple are ever-evolving. Keep praying together, keep loving one another, and keep seeking God's presence in your marriage. With faith as your foundation, your love will continue to grow and flourish, creating a lasting legacy of love, prayer, and unwavering devotion.

May your marriage be a testament to the power of love and prayer, and may God's blessings be with you on this beautiful journey of life together.

Please consider leaving a review of your experience with this book, so that other couples might find it as useful as you have:

Recommended Resources

Recommended Resources for Your Journey:

Books:

1. "The Love Dare" by Alex Kendrick and Stephen Kendrick

2. "Sacred Marriage: What If God Designed Marriage to Make Us Holy More Than to Make Us Happy" by Gary L. Thomas

3. "The Power of a Praying Husband" by Stormie Omartian

4. "The Power of a Praying Wife" by Stormie Omartian

5. "The Five Love Languages: The Secret to Love that Lasts" by Gary Chapman

Websites and Online Communities:

1. Focus on the Family (www.focusonthefamily.com)

2. FamilyLife (www.familylife.com)

RECOMMENDED RESOURCES

3. The Gottman Institute (www.gottman.com)

4. Crosswalk (www.crosswalk.com)

5. MarriageToday (www.marriagetoday.com)

Marriage Enrichment Programs and Organizations:

1. Retrouvaille (www.helpourmarriage.org)

2. Marriage Encounter (www.wwme.org)

3. Weekend to Remember (www.familylife.com/weekend)

4. The Marriage Course (www.themarriagecourse.org)

5. PREPARE/ENRICH (www.prepare-enrich.com)

Devotional Resources:

1. "The One Year Love Language Minute Devotional" by Gary Chapman

2. "Devotions for a Sacred Marriage: A Year of Weekly Devotions for Couples" by Gary L. Thomas

3. "The Love Dare Day by Day: A Year of Devotions for Couples" by Stephen Kendrick and Alex Kendrick

4. "Night Light: A Devotional for Couples" by Dr. James Dobson and Shirley Dobson

5. "The Power of Praying for Your Adult Children" by Stormie Omartian

Online Bible Study Resources:

1. Bible Gateway (www.biblegateway.com)

2. YouVersion Bible App (www.youversion.com)

3. Bible Study Tools (www.biblestudytools.com)

4. Blue Letter Bible (www.blueletterbible.org)

5. Bible.org (www.bible.org)

Online Marriage and Relationship Assessments:

1. Prepare-Enrich (www.prepare-enrich.com)

2. Love Languages Quiz (www.5lovelanguages.com)

3. Marriage Assessment Quiz (www.focusonthefamily.com/marriage/marriage-resources/marriage-assessment)

4. Gottman Relationship Checkup (www.gottman.com/how-healthy-is-your-relationship)

5. FamilyLife Marriage Assessment (www.familylife.com/marriage)

Note: These resources are provided as suggestions, and you may choose those that align best with your unique preferences and needs for continued growth in your marriage and faith.